I0105521

X-ray specs

and other vintage ads

Published in 2023 by Wolfbait Books © 2023

www.wolfbait.co.uk

ISBN: 978-1-9162151-7-7

Thanks to the following for their assistance: Andy Simons,
Rian Hughes, and Theo Powney.

A catalogue record of this book is available at the British Library.

X-ray specs

and other vintage ads

By Yahya El-Droubie

WOLFBAIT
UNDER THE COUNTER CULTURE

BLONDE IN
A BATHTUB

O ne of the many frustrations of growing up reading American comic books and magazines in the 1970s and 1980s was their tantalizing ads for such things as Sea-Monkeys and X-Ray Spex. No matter how much you were sold on their promises, and even if you did have the correct amount of pocket money, they remained out of reach across the ocean. A glow-in-the-dark monster-size skeleton could be mine if only I had dollars, and the seller would ship to the UK.

There was a parallel world of such ads aimed at "adults" to be found in the pages of men's adventure magazines, set between such articles as "Cuban Hell-Cats Scare Castro's Cutthroats" and "Weasels Ripped My Flesh."

Who wouldn't want a miniature spy camera or a permit to go wolfing while learning to draw naked ladies? If only I had a trophy room in which to hang my Mammalia Americana plaque. Would I be able to get the blonde in a bathtub to behave?

There was also plenty for the ladies, who, once furnished with their newly acquired firm bosom and wearing their teenie bikini lace panties purchased from the former burlesque dancer and stripper Lili St. Cyr, might be keen to buy a tear gas pencil to keep the wolves at bay.

The mid-20th century mail-order ads in this volume, which are largely from American publications, offer a fascinating and titillating slice of consumer history, revealing early examples of under-the-counter culture that's perhaps more brown paper envelope than brown paper bag.

Some of the ads are charmingly bizarre, and the pairing of Charles Atlas ads, such as "Girls Prefer a He-man!" alongside ads for lacy underwear can be seen as peculiar. Even stranger, however, is the tale of Harold Nathan Braunhut, the mountebank behind X-ray glasses and Sea-Monkeys.

Braunhut had a colourful past: he raced motorcycles under the name The Green Hornet and managed a showman whose act consisted of diving 40 feet into a children's wading pool filled with only 1 foot of water.

One of the items he sold was a pen-sized weapon called the Kiyoga Agent M5, which telescopes into a steel coil cosh at a flick of one's wrist. The Kiyoga caused a stink in 1988 after it was revealed in a *Washington Post* article that a portion of the sale proceeds was going to Richard Butler, founder of the neo-Nazi, white supremacists group the Aryan Nations. What made this particularly shocking at the time was the fact that Harold Nathan Braunhut, who liked using the moniker von Braunhut, was Jewish. No doubt somewhat less surprising now, what with the rise of the far right in Israel, but I digress. He also sold invisible goldfish. He died in 2003, aged 77.

The ads featured in this publication are a unique treasure chest of tease and prurient curiosity – promises from the past whose assurances still have the ability to rouse the wolf or vixen within us, despite the lives of some of their inventors.

★ ★ ★ ★ ★

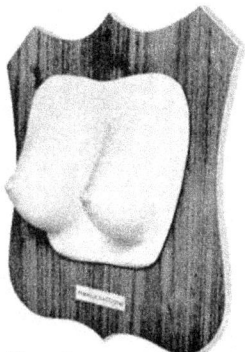

★ ★ ★ ★ ★ ★ ★ ★ ★ ★ ★

VISUAL ARTS CLUB

JEAN STRAKER'S fabulous Exhibition of classical and modern nudes
Open to the Public **DAILY** 12 - 8 p.m.—3/-

*MEETINGS EVERY EVENING for photography
and sketching with guidance for beginners.*

Membership - 1st year £3 8 0. Meeting Fees : Photography 15/-, Sketching 5/-

Studio House, 12 Soho Square, W.1

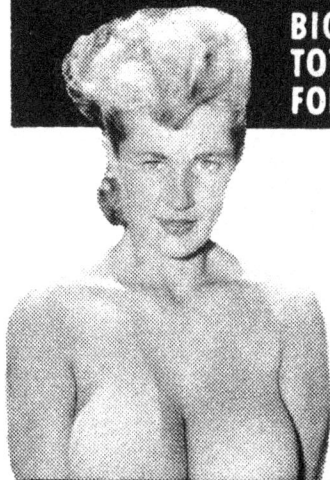

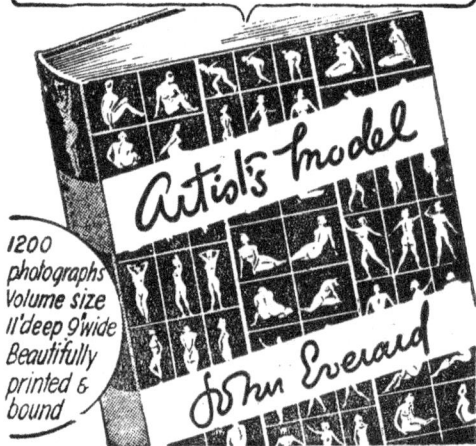

Art Model Midget Knife on Key Chain

Actual Size

Convenient Pocket Size on Chain with Your Keys

A knife that combines the beauty of a pretty girl with the convenience of a handy midget size that makes it easy to carry right along with your keys. A knife is a handy instrument to have with you and this small sized model avoids the bulky nuisance of regular sized knives. Yet its high carbon steel, full polished blade does most of the work a larger sized knife can do. Unbreakable clear plastic handle with actual art model photograph under plastic. Our illustration actual size.

Combines Beauty With Use. Handy Size

No. 8390. Price Postpaid. 65c

Hawaiian HULA Shimmy SKIRT

Imitate the Rhythm of the Natives of Hawaii!

On the beach, at masquerades, at parties, or even hanging on the wall in your bedroom or den, you will find that this Hula Skirt provides a lot of amusement. A souvenir "from the South Seas." Made of paper streamers in variegated colors.

As soon as you receive your Hula Skirt, go up to your room, put it on, and then stand before the mirror and try to imitate the rhythmic movements of the native Hawaiians. With fascinating grace you can soon learn the wiggles of the Hawaiian "shimmy," etc. Turns any gathering into a riot of fun.

No. 5706. HULA SKIRT. Adult Size. Price. 35c
No. 5702. HULA SKIRT. Children's Size.
Price Postpaid. 15c

—14—

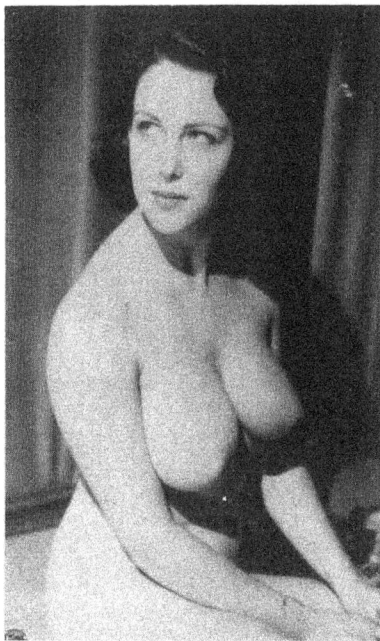

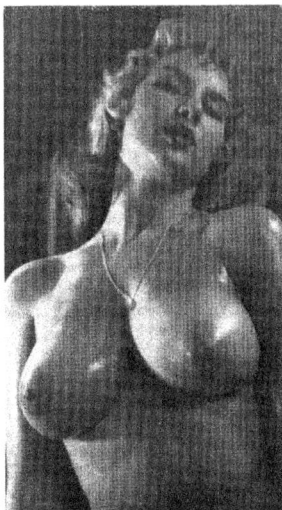

Mén! Men! Men! Men!

Everything brightens up with

Beautiful **GIRLS!**

1500 BIG GLOSSY PICTURES

MAGAZINE PHOTOS

new 24 **PAGE** *Catalogue*

BEAUTY -'OFF GUARD'

3/- WITH FREE PRINT

!

MODEL DATA LIST 1/- - - -

MAGAZINE (STUDIO 2) PHOTOS

COTTAGE GROVE, SURBITON, SURREY

SAMPLE SET - 6/-

Roger Davis

BUG EYES

**Pop Eyed
Blood-
shot**

Horrible looking, yet very realistic. slips in e y e s o c k e t like monocles. Easily held in place. In & out in a jiffy. Hole in center so you can see with them on. **39c**
No. 2063. Pair........

Can't?
Dance?

Learn the modern dances in your own home !

Send a 2½d. stamp today for 12-page booklet *Let's go Dancing* and details of our amazing ' Photostep ' Postal Course, to Dept. 150.

THE LONDON DANCE INSTITUTE,
19-23, OXFORD STREET LONDON, W.1

CHILDBIRTH
EDUCATIONAL FILM

An outstanding film of academic interest prepared for those who desire knowledge on a subject of social and medical significance.

DELIVERY BY NATURAL CHILDBIRTH

100', 8mm, B&W. Send $4.95 to National, Box 1294, San Francisco, California.

Grant's Funny Brassiere Trick

Most report that this is the laugh hit of any party or show. Can be repeated as often as desired. Get a pretty girl to step forward for a "special trick". Tell her to hold two handkerchiefs in front of her chest. When pulled, handkerchiefs suddenly change to pretty pink brassiere. And is the girl surprised and embarassed! Suggested patter for presentation with each trick that is positively full of laughs. A must! Enough said! Complete. No practise.

No. 3268. FUNNY BRASSIERE TRICK. Price Complete Postpaid....... **$3.75**

382 ★ Johnson Smith & Co., Detroit, Mich.

NATIONAL WOLFING LICENSE
Male and Female

Here is your permit to go **WOLFING**. For those who do not understand this sort of slang we will clarify the meaning of this term. It means an **ABLE GABLE** (a neat bundle of he-man), **A GOOD TIME CHARLIE** (a guy who is working the numbers racket—dating plenty of gals), **FEMALE ROBBER** (date stealer), **NECK-HAPPY** (a spooner); and in other words a **BIG TIME OPERATOR** who looks at anything. Get into the big time and start going after the gals—get your **WOLFING LICENSE.** No one can be a popular operator unless they wear this badge. Two styles; one for MALE WOLVES and one for FEMALE WOLVES. Attractively made of embossed metal. Wear it on your lapel.

No. 2041. **MALE WOLFING LICENSE.** Price Postpaid................ **15c**

No. 2042. **FEMALE WOLFING LICENSE.**
Price Postpaid.. **15c**

Calling all Men...
STRIP-TEASE NECKTIE
THAT GLOWS
IN THE DARK

"SHE LOSES HER CLOTHES AS SHE GLOWS IN THE DARK"

BY DAY

Astounding new NECKTIE is the latest rage from coast to coast! Spectacular new novelty tie creation for men who demand the distinctive and unusual! B r i n g s gasps of sheer wonder, thrilling admiration the first time you wear it! By day, smart, handsome tie that is unrivaled for sheer beauty and extravagant good looks, by night a glorious goddess of light revealed for all to see. A glorious, gleaming blonde beauty! Fully cut, Well made tie.

BY NIGHT

No. 4081. Postpaid

$1.49

PHOTOGRAPHIC STUDIES *of the* NUDE

**BOOK SIZE
11" DEEP BY
8 "WIDE**

150 pages of beautiful art plates. Interesting techniques and studies of female nudes and males in variety of poses. Full text. *Use coupon ; we will send copy.*

ON APPROVAL!

TALKING WOLF

Here is the guy who has all the girls running. **(NOT THE OTHER WAY EITHER) HE TALKS!!!** Yes and with a voice that has more come-on appeal than a beaver-haired crooner. A hot novelty. No self-respecting guy should be caught without one. Regulate speed of the talking from a "fast pitch" to a "slow drawl" and get the fast sassy dames and Southern blondes. Wonderful for bashful fellows who have trouble getting started. (The rest is up to you brother). Nearly 3-in. plastic head, with talking unit inside. Complete, nothing more needed. **35c**
No. 2897. Talking Wolf. Postpaid **35c**

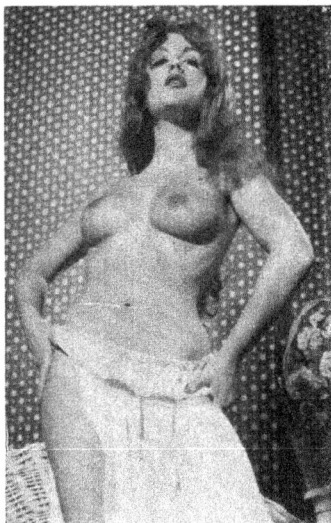

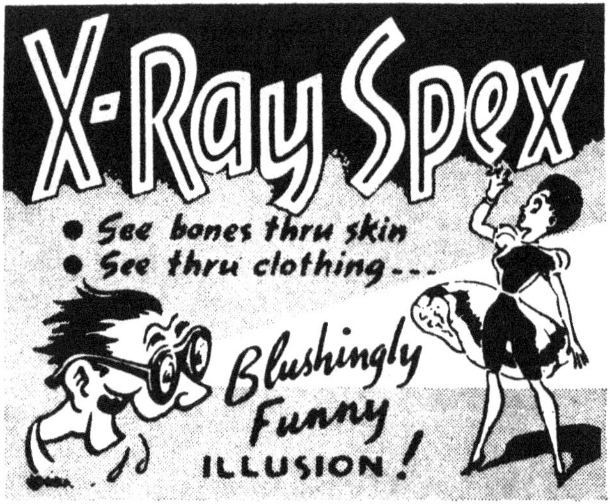

X-Ray Spex

- See bones thru skin
- See thru clothing...

Blushingly Funny ILLUSION!

ASTOUND YOUR FRIENDS WITH X-RAY VISION

ONLY

1⁹⁸

Scientific optical principle really works. Imagine — you put on the "X-Ray" Specs and hold your hand in front of you. You seem to be able to look right through the flesh and see the bones underneath. Look at your friend. Is that really his body you "see" under his clothes? Loads of laughs and fun at parties. Send only $1 plus 25¢ shipping charges or order COD and pay postman on delivery $1 plus COD shipping charges. Money Back Guarantee either way.

HONOR HOUSE PRODUCTS CORP
Lynbrook, N. Y. Dept. 52XR10

Looks and Acts Almost Alive

WIGGLES—SQUIRMS—EVEN CRAWLS. Is it alive? Looks like it. Actually seems to crawl over your hand, to the horror of all. **At the dinner table, in a restaurant, school, parties, etc., the devil's own fun.** Toss him into a carbonated drink and watch the fun. Natural brown soft rubber. **10c** **No. 2872. Famous Wig-L-Worm. Each....**

Sells Easy to Drive-Ins, Nurses, Motorists, Restaurants, Gas Stations, Stores, Banks, Homes

Discharges tear-gas to stop, stun and incapacitate the most vicious man or beast. Effective substitute for firearms. No permanent injury. No selling experience needed. Handle as a profitable sideline, soon you'll sell it full time. Start now! 5 easy sales net $25.00 a day up. Send $5.95 for complete demonstration kit of automatic Tear-Gas Pencil, 10 Demonstrators and 3 powerful Tear-Gas Cartridges. NOT SOLD TO MINORS. State age with order.

HAGEN SUPPLY CORP., Dept.G-104,St. Paul 1, Minn.

Face Appeal
for Sex Appeal

You may view a woman from the legs up, but she sees you, face first. Why look older, less exciting than you feel? Thanks to science, it is now possible to "upplift" facial contours all day or all evening. New, wonder-working SEVENTH VEIL tightens the skin, banishes lines that would otherwise show. Gone are the marks of wear and tear! Dropping jawline, under-eye puffiness and wrinkles disappear before your eyes. Takes seconds to apply. Worn day or night, gives a dependable, invisible "upplift." (So truly invisible, women swear by it!) Keeps your face young and firm.

But SEEING IS BELIEVING. Try SEVENTH VEIL and SEE the exciting change. You must look younger or pay nothing! Three months' supply, $3. SPECIAL, 2 bottles, $5. Shipped in plain wrapper. Send payment and have postage or COD. Results guaranteed.

PLAZAPLAN PRODUCTS, Dept. S-4712
225 Lafayette St., New York, N.Y. 10012

WHAT WOMEN SIGH FOR...

Romantic Lover, Jack of Hearts, Masterful Male — you're all things to all women. "Smitten," they come tearing down your doors, they won't let you go. They are yours, YOURS ALONE!

In these confidential books you'll find ancient love magic and modern sex . . . Don Juan and the Man - about - Town . . . Ways to pique wanton curiosity, win favor, make exciting love . . . Ways also to make the male personality more potent and irresistible!

For intimate and social strategy, get YOURS ALONE—2 complete books offering an Art of Love and a Way of the World. Single, engaged or married, you'll be thrilled with your new power! Only $2. Money-back guarantee.

Moaner's CRYING TOWELS

Next time any one cries about business, love, politics, bad cards, bum golf, depressions, hard luck or religion; when he says ‘ the world's "all wet" and "life simply ain't worth living," just hand him one of these Crying Towels and watch him smile through those tears. There are six paper towels in an envelope, each with the following inscription: "STOP MOANING. Dry Up Your Tears. Laugh And The World Laughs With You. Weep And You Weep Alone."
No. 2852. Crying Towels. Pkg. 6 **15c**

by RAPHAEL SOYER
WSA Collection

STUDY

ART

In Spare Time

as a way to
*a **richer** life*

DO YOU find yourself doodling interesting designs? Wanting to sketch and capture on canvas a sunny lake among the trees, or paint a likeness of a loved one? Then you should know more about the 50-year-old Washington School of Art's completely new home study Course. *In your spare time* you can learn to draw; paint in oils, water color and other media . . . all under the personal supervision of an instructor who will become your "friend by mail." Two 22-piece art outfits (a $25.00 value *at no extra cost)* will help develop your hidden talent. Learn commercial art, painting, illustrating, cartooning, fashion drawing, TV graphic art for only $6 a month!

Send for our FREE 36-PAGE BOOK and find out how little ART costs, how much it brings you. Write to **WASHINGTON SCHOOL OF ART, Studio 457, Port Washington, L. I., New York.** (Est. 1914.) *Licensed by N. Y. State Education Dept.*

Name... ....
(Please print clearly)

Address..

City.......................Zone....State...........

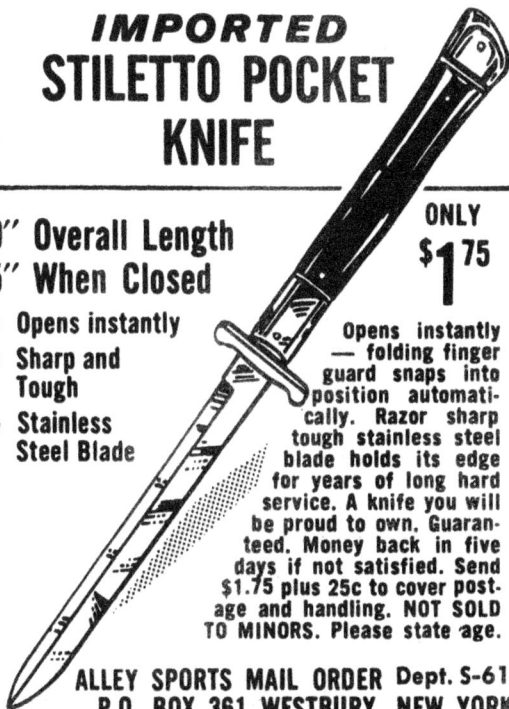

It's Sunny All The Year Round At The

WHITE HOUSE CLUB
(near Croydon)

BRITAIN'S PREMIER SUN CLUB

Are you keen to give Sunbathing a try ? And do you wish to enjoy it at its best ? Then, why not try the White House ? Run on Country Club lines, the White House aims to provide all amenities to those who wish to sunbathe, **not** back to nature, but in comfort. Vacancies exist at the moment for families, couples, single ladies, and a limited number of single men. Situated on a secluded sunny-facing hillside, it boasts a filtered swimming pool (now heated at weekends), two hard tennis courts, badminton and padder courts, and many lawns for carefree sunbathing. The twelve-bedroomed clubhouse provides all amenities for those wishing to stay. Full catering at all times. Many social activities arranged. Open all the year round. Finnish Sauna Bath—and Sun Lamps. Holiday accommodation for members only. 5 mins. from station and 35 mins. from London. Brochure giving full details sent for 2/6 P.O. from **Box 596, c/o "Health and Efficiency"**

WHOOPEE CUSHION

Blown up like a balloon and placed on a chair, couch, seat, etc. When the victim unsuspectingly sits on the cushion it gives forth noises which can be better imagined than described.

PRICE 3/-   *Postage and Packing 4d.*

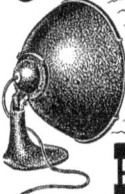

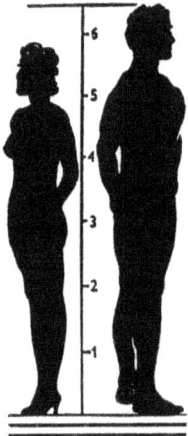

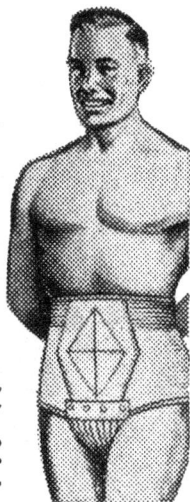

★

By John Everard —author of the famous "Artist's Model." His "Second Sitting" is even more realistically comprehensive —over 800 brilliantly produced photos, including nearly 100 full page size. The human form in every pose for photographers, artists, students, etc. Book size 11in. deep, 9in. wide, $\frac{3}{4}$in. thick, board covers.

SENT ON APPROVAL

A WINNER!

NOW YOU CAN HAVE A
FULL, FIRM NATURAL
BOSOM

*Wonderful NEW
Scientific Discovery
helps develop lovely,
womanly contour.*

Are you unhappy be-
cause your bust does not
measure up to womanly standards of beauty ?
Then you should use Kurvon, the New scientific
discovery you've been hoping and waiting for !
Kurvon is absolutely SAFE. Contains no harmful
drugs, no hormones. Yet it really works—like a
charm !

Just take Kurvon tablets as directed. Nothing
else—no massaging, no creams, no exercising, and
nothing to wear.

In 6-12 weeks you'll see your bosom blossom
into new loveliness and beauty.

Kurvon is absolutely SAFE (vide Public Analyst's
Report).

Send **30/-** for a 6 weeks' supply, or write for
FREE Brochure to :

**(Dept. H.E.), KURVON LABORATORIES,
31 North John Street, Liverpool 2**

Doctors are requested to write for free samples

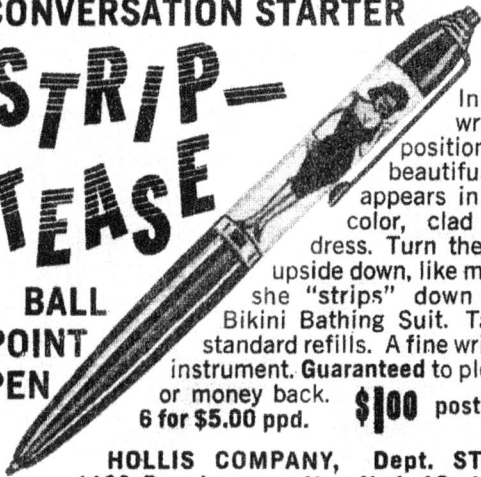

SLIMEX
home
exerciser

*the
way
top
models*

SLIM

'IT'S FUN
and so easy'

says Woman's Own

* **The Fastest Way** to a beautiful figure

* **Plus or Minus** inches where desired. For SLIMEX enables you to spot plan your figure

* **It's Medically Approved**

* **The Ideal Way** of exercising at home or out of doors, to contour the bust, shape legs, improve posture, and decrease thighs, hips and waist

* **A Model Figure** can be yours, - well proportioned, firm and supple, with a smooth rounded bust

A product of:
THE DU BARRY FIGURE RESEARCH UNIT

POST FREE

12'6

DU BARRY—London & New York Ltd.
89 Wigmore Street · London W.1

Please send ___*SLIMEX. P.O. enclosed value*___

NAME_____

ADDRESS_____

(BLOCK CAPITALS PLEASE)_____

H.E.2

—54—

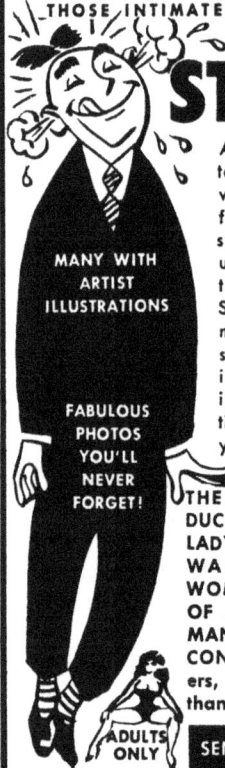

STRAIGHT FROM THE
ORIGINALS
THOSE SHOCKING
THOSE INTIMATE

STAG STORIES

A fantastic opportunity to obtain a daring, privitely printed edition featuring those rare stag story favorites you used to pass along on typewritten pages. Some you'll remember, many you've never seen, all in their original form. Every detail intact, every description vivid. They'll leave you breathless!

MANY WITH ARTIST ILLUSTRATIONS

FABULOUS PHOTOS YOU'LL NEVER FORGET!

THE MIDGET AND THE DUCHESS • THE YOUNG LADY AND HER DOG • I WAS CAPTIVE TO SIX WOMEN • DAY IN LIFE OF A TRAVELING SALESMAN • SHE STOOPS TO CONQUER, and many others, each more sensational than the next. Guaranteed!

ADULTS ONLY

Sent in Plain Wrapper. Rush cash, check or money order; no COD's!

SENSATIONAL
PRICE
LIMITED
EDITION

1 98 ppd.

PRIVATE EDITIONS
Mailing Address
BOX 69856, DEPT. P-1
LOS ANGELES 69, CALIFORNIA

"TRAVELLING LIGHT"

now available for HOME SHOWING
A shortened 8mm. version of the original
Eastmancolour production, this film was made
at a Naturist centre in Corsica and features
Yannick, the famous underwater swimmer.
(*Please see page* 5.)
8mm. SILENT only. One Reel (12 mins approx)
8mm. COLOUR £12.12. 8mm. B/W £4.10.
Please send cash with order for immediate
delivery to :—

**WALTON FILMS, Dept HE, Walton
House, 87 Richford Street, London, W.6.**

★ ★ ★ ★ ★ ★ ★ ★ ★ ★ ★

—64—

Are YOU frightened of *your* SHADOW?

HAVE you ever caught sight of your reflection in a shop window and seen your thickening shadow? Why not take steps *now* to get rid of excess fat by drinking a daily glass of hot water with a little 'Limestone' Phosphate in it? 'Limestone' Phosphate makes a delightful effervescent drink that tones up the system and flushes out food waste so that all fat forming residue is eliminated. Start taking 'Limestone' Phosphate to-day (2/3 including Purchase Tax) and make sure your shadow never grows bigger.

Be Happy, Healthy and Slim with **'LIMESTONE' PHOSPHATE**

THE MYSTIC CHARACTER THAT EVERY SERVICEMAN KNOWS

AT LAST KILROY IS HERE

Peeping Tom Is Watching You!

He's always got his eye on you and others! This likeable, nosy fellow can be worn on pocket, lapel, dress, coat, etc. Always peeking out, ready for mischief. Hand painted with screw clip.
No. 8717. PEEPING TOM. Price Postpaid............ **25c**

"Stuffed" Girl's Heads!
only $2.98

Blondes, redheads and brunettes for every man to boast of his conquests...the first realistic likeness of the exciting women who play an important part in every man's life . . . and one of the nicest qualities is that they don't talk back! Accurately modelled to three-quarters life size of real gals and molded of skin-textured pliable plastic, these heads are so life-like they almost breathe. Saucy glittering eyes, full sensuous mouth and liquid satin complexion, combined with radiant hair colors give astonishing realism to these rare and unique Trophies. Blonds, redhead or brunette mounted on a genuine mahogany plaque is complete and ready to hang on the wall for excitement and conversation. Only $2.98 plus 37¢ shipping charges. Full Money Back Guarantee. Specify Blonde, Brunette or Redhead. Send Cash, Check, or Money Order, or order C.O.D. from:

Honor House Products Corp.　　　　**Dept. MT-18**
Lynbrook, New York

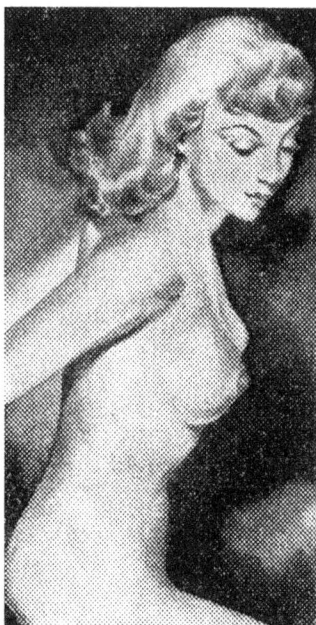

Learn **PHOTOGRAPHY** *at Home*

Prepare in spare time. Practical basic training.
Long-established school Send for free book,
"Opportunities in Photography." No obligation.

American School of Photography, 835 Diversey Pkwy., Dept. 7677 Chicago 14, Ill

Girls Can't Resist
this KISS ME NECKTIE as it
GLOWS in the DARK!

A SMART
TIE BY DAY

A MAGIC
TIE AT
NIGHT

IT'S NOVEL,
DIFFERENT
BARRELS OF
FUN!

A Beautiful Tie
.. Day and Night

Be different and the life of the party in any crowd! Here's the most amazing spectacular necktie that you ever wore, smart, wrinkle-proof, tailored cravat, which at night is a thrilling sensation! It's smart, superb class by day, and just imagine in the dark it seems like a necktie of compelling allure, sheer magic! Like a miracle of light there comes a pulsing, glowing question —Will You Kiss Me In the Dark, Baby? Think of the surprise, the awe you will cause! There's no trick, no hidden batteries, no switches or foolish horseplay, but a thing of loveliness as the question emerges gradually to life, touched by the wand of darkness, and your girl will gasp with wonder as it takes form so amazingly. A Hollywood riot wherever you go.

No. 4082. Kiss Me Tie. Postpaid **$1.49**

LEARN TO DRAW!
-earn money THIS NEW AND EASY WAY!

FREE 24-PAGE BOOK—AMAZING NEW METHOD

"OPPORTUNITIES IN ART"—a fascinating, free book containing 60 illustrations and full details of how to become a successful Commercial Artist, will prove to you that—in a matter of weeks—you can easily make startling progress and produce drawings of a standard beyond anything you had believed possible! Whatever your interest — **Cartooning, Fashion Drawing, Illustration, Figure Work, etc.,** here is a book you *must* read. and it's free!

SEND FOR THIS BOOK!

In addition to describing our new Simplified Method of learning how to draw, "OPPORTUNITIES IN ART" enables you to test this method for yourself — at once! It is all so easy . . .

- **FASHION DRAWING**
- **CARTOONING**
- **ILLUSTRATING**
- **COMMERCIAL ART, etc.**

Find out now about this fascinating hobby that can so easily lead to a worthwhile career. It may well be just what you've been looking for . . . so send for your copy of "OPPORTUNITIES IN ART" today—FREE and without obligation.

┌──FREE COUPON.──┐

Please send me your FREE book
(Write if you prefer not to cut page)

NAME.............................. ....

ADDRESS.............................

....
S.O.C. ART DEPT.
982R College House,
29/31 Wright's Lane, London. W.8

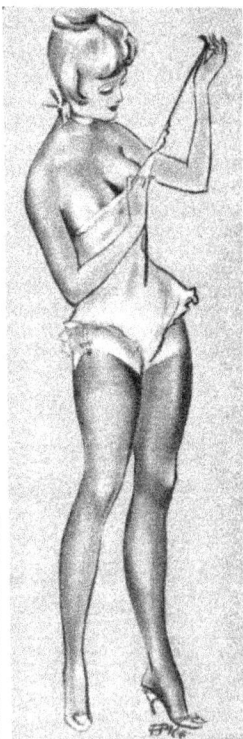

—76—

MINIATURE SECRET SPY CAMERA

only $1⁰⁰

A precision built camera that is so amazingly small it is less than 1/2 the size of a regular pack of cigarettes and can be taken everywhere you go. It weighs only 2½ ounces and is solid all-metal construction with chrome trim. It's got a professional eye level view finder and a single action 1/25th second and time exposure shutter with precision ground lens. Takes ten pictures per roll on low cost films. Makes for beautiful enlargements. So compact, it can be hidden anywhere and takes true-to-life ''spy'' pictures.

Only $1 plus 21¢ shipping charges. Six rolls of film for only 79¢. Or order C.O.D. and pay the postman on delivery plus C.O.D. charges. Full Money Back Guarantee either way.

HONOR HOUSE, DEPT. 24SP07, LYNBROOK, N. Y.

'PSYCHIC DOMINANCE

How to RULE OTHERS with your THOUGHTS.''
Full course, with stirring exercises. Illus. Adults. Only $3.
Sat. or refund. **CLARION,** Box 9309- K6 , Chicago 90

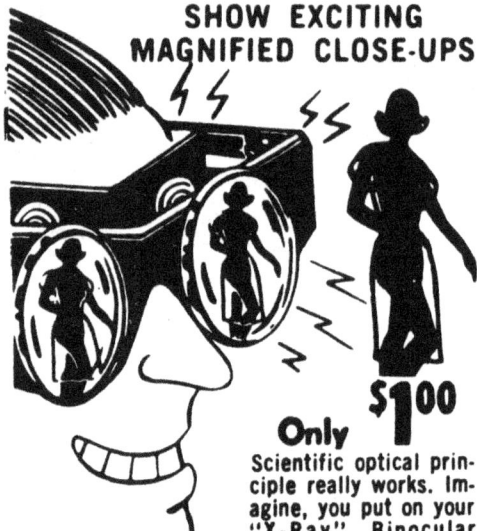

GIANT LIFE-LIKE
KARATE PRACTICE DUMMY

only 99¢

INCLUDES ILLUSTRATED KARATE INSTRUCTION PROGRAM! Now you can speed up your knowledge of KARATE and become a champ more quickly than you ever thought possible! You can practice on your own personal KARATE model—just as though you actually had a live partner to work with! Amazingly life-like Giant KARATE PRACTICE DUMMY shows clearly those vulnerable areas which should be attacked. Instantly you know WHERE to attack, while the easy-to-follow instructions included free with your KARATE MODEL show you HOW to attack. You also learn the body's major vulnerable regions, the defense or on-guard position to take, and your body's personal weapons which you can use to deadly effect, such as edge of hand, knee, elbow, etc. Big numbers on DUMMY show you exact location of pressure points and weak spots which you can practice attacking. Order your own personal DUMMY and illustrated KARATE instructions now. Check coupon.

You are in demand
if you can draw!

Make Money with your brush and pen! If you like to draw, sketch, or paint, take the famous Talent Test. No fee. No obligation. Mail this coupon TODAY!

ART INSTRUCTION, INC.
Dept. 9042 • 500 S. 4th St., Minneapolis 15, Minnesota

● Please send me your Talent Test (no fee).

Name_____Age_____

Address_____Phone_____

City_____Zone____County_____

State_____Occupation_____

DO YOU STILL BEAT YOUR WIFE?

Maybe you should never have stopped. Read why in the rollicking, provocative, yet educational booklet entitled, "Why You Should Beat Your Wife", written by an eminent practitioner of this manly art. Send 15c in stamps or coin to

CO-LE SALES COMPANY
538 W. Deming Place, Chicago 14, Illinois

GROW MONEY
IN YOUR GARDEN

£100 yearly is possible in spare time from a small plot. Save £50 on your own greengrocery and flower bills ! Make £50 selling surplus to others ! Leigh's intensive postal Course, **specially written for the amateur with a small garden or allotment,** teaches Nurserymen's methods. Develop the professional touch, get bumper crops of fresh vitamin-packed food. No special equipment or previous knowledge needed. An enthralling, health-giving, well-paying hobby.

★ COMPLETE COURSE by return post, everything you need to know,

12'6 ONLY
Money back if not delighted.

LEIGH'S SUCCESS SYSTEMS LTD. (Dept. B.1), **33, VICTORIA ROAD, SURBITON, SURREY.**

★ ★ ★ ★ ★ ★ ★ ★ ★ ★ ★

Do You Like art?

DRAW FOR MONEY!

Our Simple Method Proves You Can Learn to Draw at Home in Spare Time

YOU can learn Commercial Art, Designing, Illustrating, Cartooning, etc. . . . right at home, in spare time. No previous art training necessary. Soon be your own boss — work at home, pick your own working hours. Or earn big money as staff artist for advertising agency, newspaper, magazine, dept. store, etc. Or make Art a profitable hobby. Earn while you learn. 22-piece art outfit given with your first lesson AT NO EXTRA CHARGE. *(School est. 1914.)*

FREE BOOK, "ART FOR PLEASURE AND PROFIT." Describes our methods. Lists opportunities. Tells what our students say. No obligation. So mail coupon *at once.*

FREE BOOK

art

Beatnik Dictionary

"SWINGIN' SYLLABLES"

The Official Handbook
For Everyone In Orbit

Packed with words and phrases straight
from infinity. A perfect novelty gift.

Send One Skin (1.00)

**To: Kimbrough Pub. Co., Dept. P
4639 Poplar Ave., Memphis, Tenn.**

—96—

BUSTY WHISKEY BOTTLE COVER

Be the first to get or give this new laugh riot of home bar accessories. It's new! It's sensational! "Busty" fits over any regular 5th bottle of whiskey. She's outstanding—looks real, feels real, and is made of tough, washable plastic; hand painted in life-like color. Just moisten bottle, slip her on and she holds securely—it's that easy. Use again and again. Complete in beautiful gift box. Send only $2.00 ea. to: **NATIONAL SHOPPER, Box 69804, Los Angeles 69, California.**

Swap Neckties!

Mail us one—to—six ties you're sick of. You'll receive Pronto same number of handsomely cleaned different ties we got same way. Then you pay postman $1.

JOE'S TIE-SWAP

BOX 749   CHICAGO 90, ILLINOIS

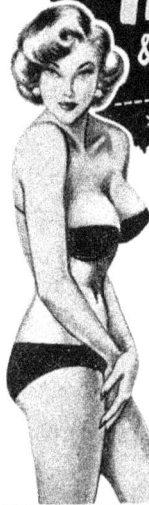

WOLFBAIT
UNDER THE COUNTER CULTURE

ALSO AVAILABLE FROM WOLFBAIT BOOKS

Doing Rude Things
The history of the British sex film.

Cinema au Naturel
A history of nudist film.

Miniten: Rules of the Game
Miniten, the tennis-like game played by naturists.

Naked as Nature Intended
The epic tale of a nudist picture by Pamela Green,
with photographs by Douglas "Dambuster" Webb, DFM.

The Naked Truth About Harrison Marks
The notorious biography by Franklyn Wood.

Past Masters of the Nude
An illustrated bibliography of nude photography
books published in England from 1896 to 1960.

Slide Show
A nostalgic look at the studio nudes of Harrison Marks.

THE STEPHEN GLASS COLLECTION

Amazons of Yesteryear
Wrestling women of the 1940s and 1950s.
A rare, action-packed collection of images.

Beauty Off-Duty
Relaxed, everyday moments caught on camera.

Naked in the Menagerie
A playful look at Eve accompanied
by her animal friends.

Nudist Camp Follies – volumes 1 and 2
An intimate look at the natural
and free atmosphere in Sun Clubs.

Nymphs and Naiads
Beauty unadorned and outdoors.

Poise and Pose
A magnificent series of photographs
of female beauty taken in the studio.

Order online at wolfbait.co.uk

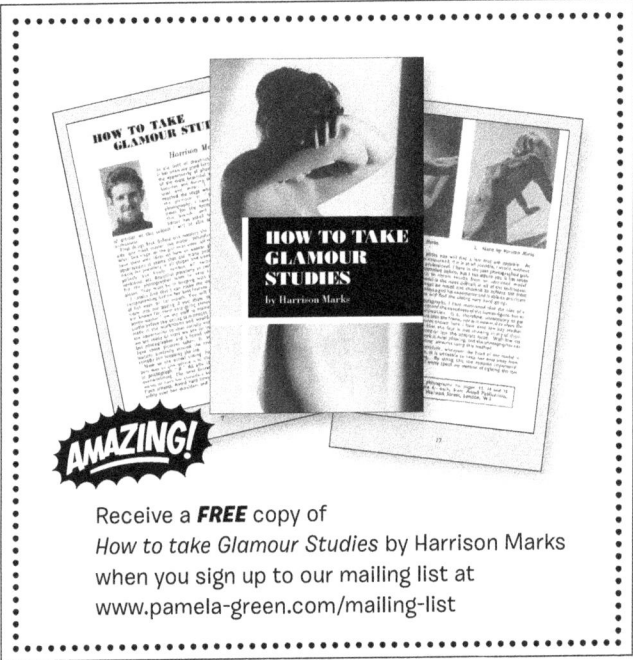

AMAZING!

Receive a **FREE** copy of
How to take Glamour Studies by Harrison Marks
when you sign up to our mailing list at
www.pamela-green.com/mailing-list

* 9 7 8 1 9 1 6 2 1 5 1 7 7 *